Exploring Artificial Intelligence: A Comprehensive Guide

John Kamau

CONTENTS

Title Page
Chapter 1 — 1
Chapter 2 — 5
Chapter 3 — 8
Chapter 4 — 11
Chapter 5 — 14
Chapter 6 — 17
Chapter 7 — 20
Conclusion — 23
About The Author — 25

CHAPTER 1
INTRODUCTION:

In the age of technological marvels, Artificial Intelligence (AI) stands at the forefront of innovation, captivating our imagination and transforming the way we live, work, and interact. From self-driving cars and intelligent personal assistants to advanced healthcare diagnostics and intricate financial algorithms, AI has become an integral part of our modern society.

This comprehensive ebook, "Exploring Artificial Intelligence: A Comprehensive Guide," invites you on a journey of discovery through the multifaceted landscape of AI. Whether you are an aspiring AI practitioner, a student fascinated by the possibilities of intelligent machines, or a business professional seeking insights into AI's potential applications, this guide is designed to equip you with a deep understanding of this groundbreaking technology.

Defining Artificial Intelligence:

Artificial Intelligence (AI) refers to the development of computer systems that can perform tasks that would typically require human intelligence. It involves the simulation of human cognitive processes such as learning, reasoning, problem-solving, perception, and language understanding. AI systems aim to analyze, interpret, and respond to complex data, adapt to changing environments, and make autonomous decisions.

Brief History of AI:

The roots of AI can be traced back to the mid-20th century when pioneers like Alan Turing and John McCarthy laid the foundations of the field. In 1950, Turing proposed the famous Turing Test, which assesses a machine's ability to exhibit intelligent behavior indistinguishable from that of a human. McCarthy, often referred to as the "Father of Artificial Intelligence," coined the term "artificial intelligence" in 1956 and organized the Dartmouth Conference, which marked the official birth of AI as a field of study.

In the early years, AI research focused on symbolic AI, also known as "good old-fashioned AI" (GOFAI), which involved programming computers with explicit rules and knowledge representation. This approach aimed to create expert systems capable of solving specific problems using logical reasoning.

During the 1980s and 1990s, AI faced challenges due to limitations in computing power and the complexity of real-world problems. However, advancements in machine learning, particularly neural networks, led to a resurgence of interest in AI in the late 1990s and early 2000s. This period witnessed breakthroughs in areas such as computer vision, natural language processing, and speech recognition.

In recent years, the availability of vast amounts of data and advancements in computational capabilities, along with the advent of deep learning, have fueled rapid progress in AI. This has led to the development of sophisticated AI applications and systems that have revolutionized various industries and domains.

Applications and Impact of AI:
AI has found applications in numerous domains, transforming industries and impacting various aspects of our lives. Some prominent applications include:
Healthcare: AI is revolutionizing healthcare by aiding in disease diagnosis, analyzing medical images, suggesting personalized treatment plans, and improving patient care and monitoring. It enables early detection of diseases, accelerates drug discovery, and enhances medical research.

Finance:
AI is reshaping the financial industry by automating tasks such as fraud detection, algorithmic trading, risk assessment, and customer service. It enhances security, streamlines processes, and enables more accurate decision-making based on real-time data analysis.

Transportation: AI is driving advancements in autonomous vehicles, optimizing traffic flow, and improving transportation safety. It enables self-driving cars, smart traffic management systems, and predictive maintenance of vehicles, leading to more efficient and sustainable transportation solutions.

E-commerce and Recommendation Systems: AI powers recommendation algorithms that personalize user experiences, leading to improved customer engagement and increased sales. AI enables targeted advertising, product recommendations, and customer sentiment analysis.

Natural Language Processing and Virtual Assistants: AI-based virtual assistants like Siri, Alexa, and Google Assistant have become integral parts of our lives, understanding and responding to natural language commands. AI enables voice recognition, language translation, chatbots, and voice-enabled smart devices.

Manufacturing and Robotics:
AI is transforming manufacturing processes through automation, predictive maintenance, and quality control. It enables collaborative robots (cobots) to work alongside humans, improving efficiency and productivity.

Education: AI is revolutionizing education by personalizing learning experiences, providing intelligent tutoring systems, and automating administrative tasks. It adapts to individual student needs, supports online learning platforms, and facilitates data-driven educational decision-making.

The impact of AI extends beyond these applications, with ongoing research and development pushing the boundaries of what is possible. However, the ethical implications of AI, such as privacy concerns, algorithmic bias, and job displacement, need to be carefully addressed to ensure responsible and beneficial deployment of AI technologies.

CHAPTER 2

TYPES OF ARTIFICIAL INTELLIGENCE:

Artificial Intelligence (AI) can be categorized into different types based on its capabilities and goals. Here are three key types of AI:

Narrow AI (Weak AI):
Narrow AI, also known as Weak AI, refers to AI systems designed to perform specific tasks or solve specific problems. These systems excel at one particular area and do not possess general intelligence or the ability to understand and perform diverse tasks like a human. Examples of narrow AI include voice assistants like Siri or Alexa, image recognition systems, and recommendation algorithms.

General AI (Strong AI):
General AI, also known as Strong AI or Human-Level AI, aims to develop AI systems capable of understanding, reasoning, and performing tasks across various domains just as a human can. General AI would possess human-like intelligence and exhibit adaptability, creativity, and a broad understanding of the world. Achieving true General AI remains a complex and ongoing challenge in the field.

Superintelligent AI:
Superintelligent AI refers to AI systems that surpass human intelligence in virtually every aspect. These hypothetical AI systems would possess cognitive abilities far beyond human capabilities and could potentially outperform humans in

intellectual tasks. Superintelligent AI is a topic of speculation and exploration, with debates surrounding its potential benefits and risks.

Symbolic AI vs. Machine Learning:
AI can also be classified based on its underlying approach to problem-solving and decision-making. Here are two prominent approaches:
Symbolic AI: Symbolic AI, also known as Classical AI or Rule-Based AI, involves representing knowledge and manipulating symbols based on predefined rules. Symbolic AI systems use logical operations to process information and derive conclusions. These systems rely on explicit knowledge representation and inference rules to solve problems. Symbolic AI was popular in the early years of AI research and is often used in expert systems and knowledge-based applications.
Machine Learning (ML): Machine Learning is an approach to AI that focuses on enabling machines to learn from data and improve performance through experience. Instead of relying on explicit rules, ML algorithms learn patterns and relationships from training data. ML models can be trained to recognize patterns, make predictions, classify data, and perform other tasks without being explicitly programmed. ML encompasses various techniques, including supervised learning, unsupervised learning, and reinforcement learning.

Supervised Learning, Unsupervised Learning, and Reinforcement Learning:
These are three primary types of learning within the field of machine learning:
Supervised Learning: Supervised learning involves training ML models using labeled data, where the input data is paired with corresponding correct output labels. The model learns from this labeled data to make predictions or classify new, unseen data accurately. The goal is to find the mapping or relationship between input and output data. Examples of supervised learning

tasks include image classification, sentiment analysis, and spam detection.

Unsupervised Learning:
In unsupervised learning, the ML model learns from unlabeled data without any predefined output labels. The objective is to identify patterns, similarities, or underlying structures within the data. Unsupervised learning algorithms can cluster similar data points together, perform dimensionality reduction, or discover hidden patterns. This type of learning is useful for tasks like customer segmentation, anomaly detection, and data exploration.

Reinforcement Learning:
Reinforcement learning involves training an agent to interact with an environment and learn through trial and error. The agent receives feedback in the form of rewards or penalties based on its actions, enabling it to learn optimal strategies and make decisions to maximize long-term rewards. Reinforcement learning is often used in scenarios such as game playing, autonomous robot control, and optimizing resource allocation.

These three types of learning provide different approaches to training ML models and enable AI systems to learn and improve their performance based on specific objectives and available data.

CHAPTER 3

MACHINE LEARNING AND DEEP LEARNING:

Machine Learning (ML) and Deep Learning (DL) are subsets of Artificial Intelligence (AI) that focus on training algorithms and models to learn from data and make predictions or decisions. Here's an overview of the fundamentals of machine learning, an introduction to deep learning, and an explanation of neural networks and deep neural networks.

Fundamentals of Machine Learning:
Machine Learning is the field of AI that involves the development of algorithms and models that can learn patterns and make predictions or decisions without being explicitly programmed. The fundamental steps in machine learning include:

Data Collection:
Gathering relevant data that represents the problem or task at hand.
Data Preprocessing:
Cleaning, transforming, and preparing the data for further analysis. This step may involve tasks like handling missing values, normalizing data, and feature engineering.

Model Selection:
Choosing the appropriate machine learning algorithm or model that best fits the problem. This selection depends on the

type of task (classification, regression, clustering, etc.) and the characteristics of the data.

Training:
Using the collected and preprocessed data to train the selected model. During training, the model learns from the data to capture patterns and relationships.

Evaluation:
Assessing the performance of the trained model using evaluation metrics to measure its accuracy, precision, recall, or other relevant metrics.

Testing and Deployment:
Applying the trained model to new, unseen data to make predictions or decisions. The model's performance is validated on this test data. Once satisfied with the performance, the model can be deployed in real-world applications.

INTRODUCTION TO DEEP LEARNING:

Deep Learning is a subfield of machine learning that focuses on training deep neural networks with multiple layers to automatically learn hierarchical representations of data. It is inspired by the structure and functioning of the human brain, specifically neural networks.

Deep Learning algorithms are capable of automatically extracting features and patterns from raw data, eliminating the need for manual feature engineering. This ability makes deep learning especially effective in tasks involving large, complex datasets, such as image and speech recognition, natural language processing, and computer vision.

Neural Networks and Deep Neural Networks:
Neural Networks are the building blocks of deep learning. They are computational models inspired by the structure and

functioning of biological neural networks in the brain. A neural network consists of interconnected layers of artificial neurons (also known as nodes or units). Each neuron receives inputs, applies weights to those inputs, performs calculations, and produces an output.

Deep Neural Networks (DNNs) are neural networks with multiple hidden layers between the input and output layers. These hidden layers enable DNNs to learn and represent complex patterns and relationships in the data. The depth of the network allows for the creation of hierarchical representations, which can capture intricate features and dependencies in the data.

Deep learning architectures, such as Convolutional Neural Networks (CNNs) for image processing and Recurrent Neural Networks (RNNs) for sequence data, have achieved significant breakthroughs in various AI applications, achieving state-of-the-art performance in areas like computer vision, natural language processing, and speech recognition.

By leveraging the power of deep neural networks, deep learning enables machines to handle increasingly complex tasks and learn intricate representations directly from the data, leading to advancements in AI capabilities.

CHAPTER 4

NATURAL LANGUAGE PROCESSING

(NLP) is a field of AI that focuses on the interaction between computers and human language. It involves understanding, interpreting, and generating human language in a way that is meaningful and useful. Here's an overview of understanding language processing, text classification and sentiment analysis, as well as speech recognition and language generation in NLP.

Understanding Language Processing:

Language processing in NLP involves various tasks aimed at enabling computers to comprehend and interpret human language. These tasks include:

Tokenization:
Breaking down text into smaller units such as words, sentences, or even characters, known as tokens.

Part-of-Speech Tagging:
Assigning grammatical tags to each word in a sentence, such as noun, verb, adjective, etc.

Named Entity Recognition:
Identifying and classifying named entities in text, such as names of people, organizations, locations, etc.

Syntax and Parsing: Analyzing the grammatical structure of sentences and establishing relationships between words.

Semantic Analysis:

Extracting the meaning and intent from text, understanding relationships between words and phrases, and interpreting context.

Text Classification and Sentiment Analysis:
Text classification is the process of categorizing text documents into predefined classes or categories. It involves training machine learning models to automatically assign categories to new, unseen texts. Examples of text classification tasks include email spam detection, sentiment analysis, topic classification, and intent recognition.

Sentiment analysis is a specific application of text classification that focuses on determining the sentiment or opinion expressed in text. It involves classifying text as positive, negative, or neutral based on the underlying sentiment. Sentiment analysis finds applications in social media monitoring, brand reputation management, customer feedback analysis, and market research.

Speech Recognition and Language Generation:
Speech recognition is the task of converting spoken language into written text. It involves processing audio signals and converting them into a textual representation. Speech recognition systems use acoustic models, language models, and machine learning techniques to transcribe spoken words accurately. Applications of speech recognition include voice assistants, transcription services, and voice-controlled systems.

Language generation, on the other hand, involves generating human-like language based on predefined rules, templates, or statistical models. This can include generating text responses in chatbots, creating automated content, and generating natural language descriptions from data. Language generation techniques can employ rule-based approaches, template-based approaches, or more advanced deep learning techniques like recurrent neural networks (RNNs) and transformers.

NLP has seen significant advancements in recent years, driven by the availability of large datasets, improvements in machine learning algorithms, and the rise of deep learning techniques. These advancements have led to the development of sophisticated NLP applications that enable better understanding, interpretation, and generation of human language, making interactions between computers and humans more natural and effective.

CHAPTER 5

COMPUTER VISION

Computer Vision is a subfield of Artificial Intelligence (AI) that focuses on enabling computers to understand and interpret visual data, such as images and videos. It involves the development of algorithms and models to extract meaningful information from visual inputs. Here's an overview of the basics of computer vision, image classification and object detection, as well as facial recognition and image generation.

Basics of Computer Vision:
Computer Vision involves the following fundamental tasks:

Image Acquisition:
Capturing visual data through various imaging devices, such as cameras or sensors.
Image Preprocessing: Cleaning and enhancing the acquired images by applying techniques like noise reduction, image resizing, and color correction.

Feature Extraction:
Extracting relevant features or patterns from the images that represent important visual characteristics. These features can be edges, corners, textures, or more complex visual attributes.

Feature Representation:
Representing the extracted features in a format suitable for analysis and further processing, such as numerical vectors or

descriptors.

Image Analysis and Understanding:
Applying algorithms and models to analyze and interpret the extracted features to understand the content, context, or semantics of the images.

Image Classification and Object Detection:
Image classification is a task in computer vision that involves assigning a label or category to an image based on its content. It is achieved by training machine learning models on labelled image datasets, where the models learn to recognize patterns and features associated with different classes. Image classification finds applications in various domains, such as autonomous driving, medical imaging, and visual search.

Object detection goes beyond image classification by not only identifying objects but also locating their positions in the image. It involves identifying and localizing multiple objects within an image using bounding boxes or other techniques. Object detection is crucial in applications like surveillance, robotics, and augmented reality.

Facial Recognition and Image Generation:
Facial recognition is a specialized application of computer vision that focuses on identifying and verifying individuals based on their facial features. It involves detecting and analyzing facial landmarks, such as eyes, nose, and mouth, to create a unique facial representation or template. Facial recognition finds applications in security systems, access control, and biometric identification.

Image generation in computer vision involves creating new images based on existing data or predefined rules. This can include generating realistic images, modifying existing images, or synthesizing new visual content. Image generation techniques range from traditional methods like image manipulation and texture synthesis to advanced deep learning approaches like generative adversarial networks (GANs) and variational autoencoders (VAEs).

JOHN KAMAU

Computer vision has made significant progress in recent years, driven by advancements in deep learning algorithms, increased computing power, and the availability of large annotated image datasets. This has led to the development of advanced computer vision systems capable of understanding and interpreting visual information, opening up new possibilities in areas such as autonomous vehicles, medical imaging diagnosis, and visual content analysis.

CHAPTER 6

AI AND ETHICS

As Artificial Intelligence (AI) continues to advance and permeate various aspects of our lives, it raises important ethical considerations. Understanding and addressing these ethical implications is crucial to ensure the responsible and beneficial development and deployment of AI technologies. Here are three key areas of ethical concern in AI: the ethical implications of AI, bias and fairness in AI systems, and privacy and security concerns.

ETHICAL IMPLICATIONS OF AI:

AI systems have the potential to impact society in profound ways, and their development and use should be guided by ethical principles. Some key ethical implications of AI include:

Transparency and Explainability: AI systems should be transparent, providing explanations for their decisions and actions. Understanding the reasoning behind AI-generated outcomes is crucial for building trust and accountability.

Accountability and Responsibility:
As AI systems make decisions and take actions, it is important to establish accountability and assign responsibility for any potential harm caused by those systems. Clear lines of responsibility and legal frameworks need to be developed to address AI-related issues.

Impact on Employment:
AI technologies have the potential to automate certain jobs and tasks, leading to job displacement and economic disruption. Ensuring a just and equitable transition for workers affected by AI-driven automation is essential.

Bias and Fairness in AI Systems:
AI systems can inadvertently perpetuate biases and unfairness present in the data used to train them. Some considerations regarding bias and fairness in AI systems include:

Data Bias: AI algorithms learn from historical data, which may contain biases and reflect societal prejudices. If these biases are not addressed, AI systems can perpetuate discrimination or unfair treatment. Careful data selection and preprocessing, as well as regular auditing of AI models, are necessary to mitigate bias.

Fairness in Decision-Making: AI systems should strive for fairness in decision-making, treating individuals equitably and avoiding discrimination based on sensitive attributes such as race, gender, or socioeconomic status. Fairness metrics and techniques need to be developed and implemented in AI systems to mitigate biases and ensure equitable outcomes.

Privacy and Security Concerns:
AI technologies often involve the collection, processing, and analysis of vast amounts of personal data, raising privacy and security concerns. Key considerations in this area include:

Data Privacy: AI systems must handle personal data in a privacy-preserving manner, adhering to relevant data protection regulations. Collecting only necessary data, implementing data anonymization techniques, and ensuring secure data storage and transmission are crucial to protect individuals' privacy.

Security Risks: AI systems can be vulnerable to malicious attacks, posing risks to data integrity, system reliability, and public safety. Robust cybersecurity measures, including encryption, access controls, and regular security audits, are essential to protect AI systems from unauthorized access and attacks.

Ethical Use of Data: AI developers and organizations must ensure that the data used to train AI models is obtained and used ethically and legally. This involves obtaining informed consent, respecting data ownership rights, and preventing unauthorized data access or misuse.

Addressing these ethical implications requires collaboration among AI researchers, policymakers, industry leaders, and society at large. Ethical frameworks, regulations, and guidelines are being developed to promote responsible AI development and usage, ensuring that AI technologies are aligned with human values and societal well-being.

CHAPTER 7

THE FUTURE OF ARTIFICIAL INTELLIGENCE

Artificial Intelligence (AI) is a rapidly evolving field with the potential to revolutionize various industries and aspects of human life. Here are some key aspects related to the future of AI: advances in AI research, AI and automation, and possibilities and limitations of AI.

Advances in AI Research:

AI research continues to push the boundaries of what machines can achieve. Some areas of advancement include:

Deep Learning and Neural Networks:

Deep learning techniques, particularly neural networks, have made significant strides in solving complex problems by enabling machines to learn from vast amounts of data. Ongoing research focuses on improving model architectures, training algorithms, and transfer learning to enhance the performance and efficiency of neural networks.

Reinforcement Learning:

Reinforcement learning, a form of machine learning that involves learning through interaction with an environment, holds promise for training AI agents to make optimal decisions in dynamic and uncertain situations. Advancements in reinforcement learning algorithms, such as model-based approaches and exploration strategies, are driving progress in autonomous systems and robotics.

Explainable AI:
The need for transparency and interpretability in AI systems has gained attention. Research is being conducted to develop techniques that provide explanations for AI-generated decisions, enabling users to understand and trust AI systems. This area of research aims to address the "black box" problem and make AI more understandable and accountable.

AI and Automation:
AI is poised to revolutionize automation across various industries, impacting the future of work and productivity. Key considerations include:
Increased Efficiency and Productivity: AI technologies, such as robotic process automation, machine learning algorithms, and natural language processing, can automate repetitive and mundane tasks, leading to increased efficiency and productivity. This allows human workers to focus on more creative and complex tasks, driving innovation and value creation.
Job Displacement and Reskilling: The automation potential of AI raises concerns about job displacement. While certain tasks may be automated, new job roles and opportunities may also emerge. Reskilling and upskilling the workforce will be crucial to adapt to the changing job landscape and ensure individuals can leverage AI technologies effectively.

Possibilities and Limitations of AI:
While AI holds immense potential, it also has certain limitations and challenges:
Ethical Considerations: As AI becomes more prevalent, ethical considerations surrounding AI decision-making, bias, privacy, and accountability become increasingly important. Striking a balance between technological progress and ethical considerations will be crucial to ensure AI benefits society as a whole.
General AI and Consciousness: The development of General AI, which possesses human-level intelligence across various

domains, remains a challenge. The quest for achieving AI systems with human-like consciousness or self-awareness raises fundamental questions and philosophical debates.

Data Availability and Quality: AI relies heavily on large and high-quality datasets for training and performance. Access to diverse and representative data can be a challenge, particularly in domains with limited data availability or biased datasets. Ensuring data privacy, security, and quality are ongoing concerns.

Robustness and Safety: Ensuring AI systems are robust, reliable, and safe is critical. Addressing issues such as adversarial attacks, system failures, and unintended consequences of AI decision-making requires ongoing research and development of safety mechanisms.

As AI continues to advance, interdisciplinary collaboration, ethical frameworks, and responsible deployment will be vital for harnessing its potential while addressing its limitations and ensuring its positive impact on society. The future of AI holds tremendous promise for transformative advancements in various fields, driving innovation, and enhancing human capabilities.

CONCLUSION

The future of AI is filled with possibilities and potential, but it also comes with challenges and responsibilities. As AI continues to advance, it is essential to ensure that its development and deployment align with ethical principles and human values. Striving for fairness, transparency, and accountability is crucial to build trust and mitigate potential biases and risks.

Collaboration among researchers, policymakers, industry leaders, and society at large is vital for shaping the future of AI in a way that benefits humanity. With responsible development, AI has the potential to transform industries, enhance human capabilities, and tackle complex global challenges.

As we embark on this exciting journey of AI, let us remain mindful of the ethical considerations, strive for inclusivity and fairness, and leverage the power of AI to create a better future for all.

ABOUT THE AUTHOR

John Kamau

John is a seasoned AI researcher and technology enthusiast with a passion for exploring the frontiers of Artificial Intelligence. With a background in computer science and extensive experience in machine learning,Cyber security and data analytics, John has been actively involved in AI research and development for over a decade. John is dedicated to sharing his knowledge and insights with others, making complex AI concepts accessible and understandable. He has conducted workshops and training programs to empower individuals and organizations with the knowledge to leverage AI effectively.

www.ingramcontent.com/pod-product-compliance
Lightning Source LLC
Chambersburg PA
CBHW030045230526
45472CB00005B/1691